A home for Little Teddy

By Beverley Randell
Illustrated by Chantal Stewart

"I can not sleep here,"
said Little Teddy.
"Where can I sleep?"

Little Teddy went to look
for a home.

He went to see the mouse.

"Can I come in?"
said Little Teddy.
"I am looking for a home."

"No," said the mouse.
"You can not come in.
This is a home for mice."

Little Teddy went away.

7

He went to see the rabbit.

"Can I come in?"
said Little Teddy.
"I am looking
for a home."

"No," said the rabbit.
"You can not come in.
This is a home for rabbits."

Little Teddy went away.

Little Teddy went
to see the little dolls.
"Can I come in?" he said.
"I am looking for a home."

The dolls looked
at Little Teddy.

"Come in, Little Teddy," said the dolls.
"You can sleep up here, in this little bed."

"Oh, **thank** you," said Little Teddy.

15

"This is a good home for a little teddy!"